Gunié in Wonderland

Shusha Dao
Illustrated by Daichi Hayashi

三省堂書店／創英社

I

December 25th was a special day for Gunié Zaitoh not only because it was Christmas but also because it was her birthday. Every year, she had received toys or picture books as presents from her family and relatives. But she would become ten years old within a few weeks. She wanted more grown-up presents for her coming birthday.

When Gunié's father Dagaji asked her what she would like to have for her birthday, she asked him to buy an interesting yet difficult book for her. After thinking for a while, Dagaji said, "OK. Let's go to my favorite bookstore on Christmas Eve together. You can choose one book which looks interesting yet difficult there."
Gunié agreed.

On the 24th of December, 2019, Gunié and Dagaji went to the bookstore named 'Bookworms' Paradise'. There were at least ten thousand books inside the shop. Her father told her to find the book which she would like to read. She walked and walked, looking for a catchy title. Finally, she found a book named '*Gunié in Wonderland*'. She liked the book because the name of the main character of the book seemed the same as hers. Dagaji bought the book for her. She promised Dagaji that she would read, starting on her birthday, at least 3 pages but no more than 5 pages per day. As such she would be able to finish reading the book by 4th of May: Dagaji's birthday.

II

Two weeks have passed since Gunié started reading the book. The age of the protagonist was not written, but perhaps *Gunié* was at least 7 years older than she. What she had not expected was that *Gunié* was not a girl but a boy!

Gunié had just finished the second chapter of the book. For some reason, *Gunié* was chosen to play a role as a time traveler. His mission was to carry a time capsule to several cities in several eras and hide it in one of the most famous buildings of each city. In the chapter 1, *Gunié* went to Cairo in the 26th century BC and hid a capsule inside the Great Pyramid of Giza. In the chapter 2, he traveled to Rome in the 1st century AD and hid another capsule inside the Colosseum. The stories were always full of adventures. From the following day, Gunié would start reading the chapter 3. She was really looking forward to it.

That night *Gunié* happened to appear in her dream. He seemed a bit younger than she had imagined.

"Hey, can you help me? I'm totally confused," said *Gunié*. Gunié was so surprised that she could not say anything.

Then, she woke up from a dream.

III

When Gunié read the first page of the chapter 3, she learned *Gunié*'s next destination would be Paris, the capital of France. He went to the city in the 1880's. At first, *Gunié* was planning to hide the time capsule inside the Eiffel Tower. But when he arrived at the place, he knew that the tower was still under construction. He therefore had to change his idea. He decided to hide the capsule inside Notre-Dame de Paris.

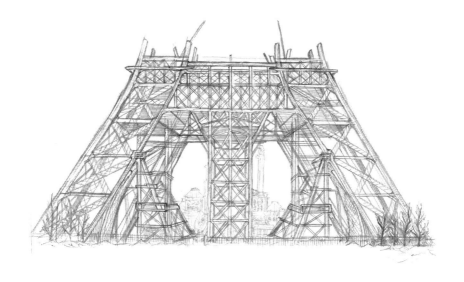

As was usual, *Gunié* said a magic word '*Shabberwocky*' at the end of the chapter in order to go back. The magic word created a tremendous noise, and he returned to his original place whose name was not written.

"Where does he live? And 'when' is he from?" wondered Gunié.

On the 18th of January, *Gunié* appeared in her dream again. She was not surprised at his appearance then.

"Are you still confused?" asked Gunié.

"Yeah. I'm still in a panic," answered *Gunié*, "I don't know why, but I forgot how to go back to my place."

Gunié thought about '*Shabberwocky*'. But she did not want to tell him the magic word.

"Explain more. I might be able to help you find the way to go back."

IV

"I came here to Tokyo two days ago," *Gunié* started talking.

"At first I thought I would hide my capsule inside the Tokyo Tower. But I had to check if the Tokyo Tower is still famous in the 2020's. Because this is my first time travel to the future."

"You came here from the past!" Gunié interrupted.

"Yeah. And so I asked some people if they knew the Tokyo Tower and they did. But many of them said they liked Tokyo Skytree better. So I decided to go to Tokyo Skytree instead of the Tokyo Tower."

"And then?"

"And I hid the capsule inside the tower. But soon after that, I had a terrible headache and had to lie on a bench. I slept for a while, woke up, and forgot how to travel back to my era."

"Don't you remember how to go back at all?" asked Gunié.

Gunié sighed.

"Maybe I have to say a secret word. But I have no idea what it is."

"I think I know the word. It is '*Nabberyocky*'," Gunié lied.

Gunié's face lit. He looked very happy.

"Yeah. The word rings a bell. Thank you so much for your help. Let's meet again sometime somewhere. Good bye!" said *Gunié* and shouted, "*Nabberyocky!*"

All of a sudden, *Gunié* started getting smaller and smaller. Finally, he disappeared.

V

"How are you doing with the book?" asked Dagaji during breakfast.

It was already in mid-February. Gunié was supposed to finish the chapter 8 of '*Gunié in Wonderland*' in a couple of days.

"I enjoy reading it," she replied absently.

The book was still interesting to read and *Gunié* was always energetic and adventurous. From the chapter 4 to the chapter 7, he went to Agra, New York, Rio de Janeiro, and Berlin in the several eras and hid a capsule inside the Taj Mahal, the Empire State Building, Christ the Redeemer, and the Brandenburg Gate, respectively. In the chapter 8, *Gunié* went to Sydney in the late 1970's and caught a cold: he thought it would be summer in August in Sydney and went there with a T-shirt. Gunié also learned what were inside the time capsule: some coins, an envelope with a letter inside, and a calendar.

Since she told a lie to *Gunié*, however, Gunié could not enjoy the book as before. Knowing that had happened in her dream, she felt guilty towards him.

"Wait. Was it really a dream?" Gunié sometimes asked to herself.

"...nié; Gunié, are you listening to me?" asked Zaori, her mother.

"Sorry, what did you say, Mom?"

"I said, let's go to Tokyo Skytree this afternoon."

VI

"Look at Mount Fuji! Look at the shadow of this tower!

Wow, what a beautiful scenery!" shouted Zaori.

It was a cold yet clear day, with no single cloud in the sky.

"It is...," nodded Dagaji, keeping a distance from the windows. He was scared of heights.

It was the first time to visit Tokyo Skytree for Zaitoh family. Unlike her mother who was acting like a child, however, Gunié was walking slowly in the observation deck, watching the floor carefully.

"Don't look down, but look out of window, Gunié," laughed Zaori, "there's nothing special on the floor."

Gunié thought there could be something on the floor. Something like a capsule might be found. She did not pay attention to the outside the deck. Her parents were a little sad to know she was not interested in the visit.

Zaori and Dagaji decided not to stay inside the tower for a long time.

"Let's go down in a couple of minutes. Or Dad will faint with fear of heights," Zaori joked.

Gunié wanted to remain in the deck longer, but followed their decision.

After waiting for their turn for a while, they got on the elevator. Gunié stared blankly at the deck before the elevator doors closed.

Suddenly, Gunié saw a boy passing the elevator from right to left. He seemed to hold a capsule-like item in his arms.

"What have I just seen?" murmured Gunié.

Then, the doors closed.

VII

Gunié stopped reading '*Gunié in Wonderland*'. She could not bring herself to finish the chapter 8. If she did it, she would need to move to the chapter 9. And what if *Gunié*'s next destination was Tokyo...? Somehow she was scared.

Gunié never appeared in her dream again.

Her parents were aware that Gunié had suddenly stopped reading. They were worried, but they believed that she would start reading the book again someday.

Tokyo Skytree was closed because of COVID-19. Even if she wished, she would not be able to enter the tower.

"Well, I need to do something else for a change," said Gunié to herself.

One day, Gunié and Maja Ibamoto, her best friend, took part in a special after-school event. The main topic of the event was how to make Tokyo more attractive. All the participants of the event had to do a study about Tokyo as their homework. So the two girls decided to find out several different ways to go to Tokyo Station from Ueno Station and compare advantages and disadvantages of each method.

VIII

Teachers of the special after-school event liked Gunié and Maja's report very much. Although the next special event was canceled because of the pandemic, Gunié wanted to study something more.

Due to COVID-19, her school itself was closed, too. Not knowing what to do with her free time, one day she went to Ueno Station – the nearest station from her house – and started counting the number of vending machines in the area.

"One, two, three..."

It was too difficult for Gunié to count them all because Ueno Station was huge. After 40 minutes, she decided to take a rest and sat on a bench.

She watched people walking in the station. Many of them were wearing a mask. There was a kiosk just 10 meters away from her, in which small Miraitowa and Someity dolls were sold. Gunié wondered if 2020 Olympics would be really held that year.

Suddenly, she spotted a young boy who was walking hurriedly. He carried a capsule-like item!

"He must be *him*," said Gunié to herself and stood up.

She started running and followed him. She had missed him in Tokyo Skytree. She should not miss him again.

"*Gunié, Gunié,*" shouted Gunié.

Finally, she caught up with him and grabbed his arm.

"*Gunié!*"

The boy looked back at her.

IX

"How come you're calling your own name, Gunié?" said the boy.

The boy was not *Gunié* she had seen in her dreams.

"How do you know my name?" asked Gunié.

"Because you have a name plate here," smiled the boy.

She covered the name plate with her hands and blushed.

"Never mind. By the way, I'm Biro. Nice meeting you."

"Nice to meet you, Biro."

"Now back to my question. Why did you say your name and speak to me?"

"Because...," Gunié hesitated, "because I thought you were *Gunié*, I mean, nothing. I simply made a mistake. Sorry."

"Oh, OK. Don't worry. Everyone makes a mistake. Now I have to go. Bye!"

"Wait, Biro. What is the capsule you hold?" asked Gunié.

"Capsule? Haw-haw! No, this is not a capsule," replied Biro, "this is special stuff for something like a muscle training. I'm always with this when I walk outside. Always. I'm a kind of gymnast."

Gunié was a bit puzzled yet relieved.

"Sorry, I know you're in a hurry, Biro, but one more question. Were you in Tokyo Skytree a couple of weeks ago?"

"I was! How do you know?"

X

"The boy I saw in Tokyo Skytree was not *Gunié*!"

Gunié felt as if she had been freed from guilt.

She told Maja what had happened to her in the past month: her two dreams, her visit to Tokyo Skytree, and her experience in Ueno Station.

"That's why you looked nervous these days," said Maja.

"Did I look nervous?"

"Absolutely. You stopped talking about the book. You sighed every one minute when we were together. Why didn't you tell me earlier?"

"Because... because I just couldn't," said Gunié, "I thought my story was too unrealistic for you to believe."

"Oh, Gunié. No worries. Look. I sometimes become a mermaid and swim in the sea in my dream! From now on, tell me whatever when you are worried, OK?"

"I will," nodded Gunié. She was happy to have such a nice friend.

"By the way, did Biro tell you his family name?" asked Maja.

"No. He said only his first name. Why?"

"Um... If his name is Biro Biroda, he goes to the same high school as Agira's."

"Is Biro Biroda Agira's friend?"

"Not exactly. He's one year senior to my big bro. I know him because he's famous."

XI

According to Maja, Biro Biroda was a member of Cirque de la Nature and performed acrobatic feats. On the following day, she brought a photo of the acrobat to Gunié's place.

"Does this ring a bell ?" asked Maja excitedly.

The boy was disguised as a clown on the photo.

"No, Maja. I don't think this is Biro I met," answered she.

Gunié restarted '*Gunié in Wonderland*'. As she had plenty of time, she changed the rule about reading from then on: she could read more than five pages a day if she wanted, she would not have to read it everyday, she could not read different chapters in one day, and her reading time per day could not exceed one hour and a half.

Gunié finished reading the rest of the chapter 8 on the same day.

XII

Gunié closed the book immediately after she knew *Gunié*'s destination of the chapter 9 would be Tokyo. She was sweating with fear.

"Where in Tokyo is *Gunié* going to hide the capsule?" After trying to calm herself down for a while, she grabbed the book and went to the kitchen where Zaori had just begun to prepare supper.

"Mom, can you do me a favor?" asked Gunié.

"Sure. What can I do for you?"

Gunié opened the book and showed its page 194 and 195 to her mother.

"I want you to tell me what you see on these pages."

"Well, I see many words," smiled Zaori.

"I mean," Gunié stammered, "can you find any keywords like a place name?"

"Let me see... I see the word 'Tokyo'."

"Just 'Tokyo'? Then it's not important. What else can you see?"

"Hmmm, ...how about 'the 14th century AD'?"

Gunié's face lit.

"Awesome! Thanks so much, Mom! Sorry I can't help you now, but I'll do the dishes after dinner. I promise!"

Gunié went back to her room and opened the book again.

XIII

No doubt, neither Tokyo Skytree nor the Tokyo Tower existed in the 14th century AD.

"*Gunié* will go somewhere else, but where?" wondered Gunié.

The answer was written on the page 203. It was indeed one of the most famous buildings of the era: Senso-ji in Asakusa. But before hiding the capsule, *Gunié* had to consider the famous temple's possible destruction in the 'future'. He time-traveled

back to his 'era' in order to check Senso-ji's 'history', and
learned that the temple had been burnt out several times between
14th and 20th century. He therefore decided to dig up the yard
behind the Five-Story Pagoda and hide the capsule in the soil.
Gunié traveled to the place in the 14th century again and started
digging.

The chapter 9 was a long one. Gunié wanted to finish the
chapter before supper in vain: the alarm clock to inform her

daily reading time limit rang.

She stopped the alarm clock, closed the book, and went to the dining room.

XIV

Gunié knew that she would finish reading the chapter 9 in a few pages. Since she made it a rule not to read different chapters in one day, she preferred to read the book at night before she slept. Her school was still closed: it was on spring holidays. She had too much free time, but she did not bring herself to go out because of the bad weather.

Luckily, Maja visited her house. She suggested they should study more about Tokyo attraction. The two girls searched for interesting spots near their houses using Internet, and decided to widen their knowledge of Ueno Park. They promised to meet at the Tokyo National Museum on the following day and Maja left for home.

After changing into her pajamas, Gunié put the book on the bedside table, turned off the room light, turned on the bedside lamp, and started reading the rest of the chapter in the bed. She was so sleepy that she could not read as fast as she usually did. Finally, *Gunié* in the story finished hiding the capsule. The chapter was almost over. When her eyelids were about to close, however, Gunié noticed that something was rewritten by hand at the bottom of the page.

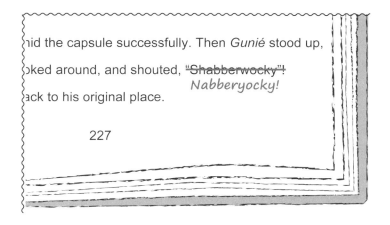

She got chills down her spine.

XV

"Fire away," said Maja with a grave look.

Gunié and Maja were in front of the Tokyo National Museum, which was closed.

"Sorry, Maja?"

"You have to tell me something. You look so different from yesterday."

"Do I?"

"Don't be silly. Something must have happened after I left your house."

Gunié remained silent for a while, and opened her mouth.

"You won't believe me."

"Yes, I'll believe you," said Maja. "I told you everything is possible in a dream."

"No, Maja.... It is not about what happened in my dream," uttered Gunié and started sobbing.

Now it was Maja's turn to remain silent for a while.

"Well, Gunié.... I have to be honest. I can't really guarantee I'll believe your story. But I'll try to. Share your problem with me."

XVI

After she heard what Gunié had seen in the book, Maja said,

"Let's go to Senso-ji now. It's within a walking distance

from here."

Without waiting for her reply, she grabbed Gunié's arm and started heading for the temple. Overwhelmed by Maja's restless energy, Gunié could not do anything but follow her.

They arrived at Senso-ji. Although the weather was better than the previous day, the sky looked – at least to Gunié – heavy gray.

Not many visitors were there: Hanami season was almost over.

"Let's go behind the Five-Story Pagoda," said Maja.

Nobody was there.

"Oops, I should have brought a magnet."

"Why, Maja?"

"The capsule contains some coins, right? If we search for the capsule using a magnet, we may hear the coins moving inside the soil."

"Are you trying to find a capsule?" Gunié felt intimidated.

"Why not? That could clear the mystery, couldn't it?"

"No," said Gunié, "things wouldn't go so smoothly."

Gunié took a few steps backward to show her reluctance.

All at once, Gunié felt as if she had got an electric shock and crouched down.

"What happened?" asked Maja and stepped close to her.

She was trembling and out of breath. After a minute, she raised her face and whispered, "listen, Maja. I'm sure the capsule is just below me."

XVII

"Stay here. Don't move until I'm back," said Maja and ran away.

After a couple of minutes, she came back with two brooms.

"Where did you get them from?"

"Never mind. Now let's dig the soil together."

Using the handle part of the brooms, the two girls dug the ground. There were some people passing the yard, but nobody paid attention to them. After ten minutes or so, Gunié felt something hard inside the dirt through the broom.

"This is the one," said Gunié.

They continued and finally succeeded in digging up a capsule. They wiped off the soil on the surface of the capsule and opened it. As was written in the book, there were some coins, an envelope, and a calendar inside.

"Let's read a letter."

Urged by Maja, Gunié opened the envelope, took the letter and unfolded it.

> I'm waiting for you, Gunié.

At that moment, Gunié stretched her back and raised her hands as if under a magic spell, and shouted, "*Nabberyocky!*"
Maja saw Gunié getting smaller and smaller. Finally, she disappeared.

XVIII

Biro Biroda was upset when he was asked by a policeman to go to the nearest kōban on his way back. He had to remain seated on a chair in the police box station until another policeman came there with an egg-shaped item. Not only the shape but the size of the item looked exactly the same as the kit Biro carried on that day, as was usual.

"Do you have any idea of this?" said one of the policemen.

"Well, at least it has nothing to do with this," replied Biro angrily.

What Biro always carried was, actually, made of special metal.

"We don't suspect you nor are we going to arrest you," said another policeman, "we are merely trying to find a clue about this."

"Is it openable?" asked Biro.

"Yes. We've already opened it and found a calendar and 500-yen coins inside."

"How did you get it?"

"In fact, a girl at around ten years of age brought this."

Biro remembered the girl he had met at Ueno Station.

"Does the name of the girl happen to be Gunié or something?"

"No. It is Maja. She just said her name and ran away without leaving her address."

For whatever reason, Biro felt a sense of responsibility to solve the mystery.

"Sirs, can I keep this item for a while? I might be able to identify the girl who brought this."

Around the same time, Dagaji found in his mailbox a message note in an envelope, which said:

Dear Mr. Zaitoh,

Please don't worry. Your daughter will be back on your birthday.

Read 'Gunié in wonderland' from the chapter 10 until the end by then.

The sender's name was not written either on the envelope or on the note.

XIX

Biro took a calendar from the item he had brought home and observed it. Strangely, there was no description of the year on it. The first of January fell on Tuesday. He took his smartphone and opened the schedule app.

"This is the calendar of 2019, last year," said Biro to himself.

He gazed at three 500-yen coins inside the item. He wondered what could be purchased with 1,500 yen. Then he put his metal kit next to it. Although the former was much heavier than the latter, the two items looked extremely similar.

Feeling at a loss, Biro threw his body on the bed, and fell into a deep sleep before he knew.

Biro lived in a small apartment offered by Cirque de la Nature which he belonged to. He had spent his early years in an orphanage. When he was twelve years old, a clown of the circus paid a visit to the orphanage for charitable activities. The clown's backflip was so inspiring that many children wanted to try to mimic it.

After one week, the clown came to the facility again to give a backflip lesson.

"Alright, everyone. Let's practice on this mat. Who wants to start?"

The clown helped each child do a backflip-like movement by supporting his or her body. The atmosphere of the lesson was cheerful with constant laughter until Biro's turn came. When he stood on the mat, everyone got an overwhelming vibe from him and remained silent. Then Biro did a back somersault by himself. After a moment of silence, he got thunderous applause.

Later on that day, Biro was 'headhunted' by the clown.

XX

When Dagaji finished reading the chapter 10 of '*Gunié in Wonderland*', he was convinced that the sender of the message note was a trustworthy person. He told the story of the chapter to Zaori, who showed a satisfied look on her face.

"Do you have any idea of who sent you the message?" asked she.

"Not at all. But we'll know before long. Don't you think so?"

Zaori nodded and said, "and it was not the strangest message you'd ever received, was it?"

XXI

"Hello again, Gunié," said *Gunié*.

Gunié was still in the backyard of the Five-Story Pagoda of Senso-ji.

"Why are you here? Where's Maja? What the heck is going on?"

She was totally confused.

"Don't worry," said he gently, "we're in Tokyo in 2030."

"Am I in the future?"

"Yes, but we need to time-travel again right now."

"Why? Why do we have to?"

Gunié sighed deeply.

"Because there exist Gunié at the age of twenty here in 2030. If you accidentally meet her, it's going to be troublesome."
Gunié was still confused.

"Let's go anyway. We must leave now." *Gunié* grabbed her left arm and shouted, "*Shabberwocky!*"
They instantly disappeared with a tremendous noise.

XXII

"Welcome Gunié to my original era!" said *Gunié*.
Gunié looked around. They were still in the same place.

"'When' are we now?"

"You'll see. Let's walk a little for now."
They headed for Asakusa Station.
When they reached the bank of the Sumida River, Gunié noticed that Tokyo Skytree could not be seen.

"Do we happen to be in the 14th century?" she asked.

"Hey, calm yourself down. We've just passed close by Asakusa Station, right? It didn't exist in the 14th century."
Gunié thought his explanation made sense.

"So when in the world am I now?"
Gunié smiled and said proudly, "you're in 1985, Gunié."

"My dad was born in 1985. I want to see him being a baby!" Gunié said excitedly.

"Oh, I forgot about it! No, Gunié, you can't. Just as you couldn't see yourself in 2030, it is impossible to see your family here now. Do you have any siblings?"

"No..."

"Is your mother younger than your father?"

"Yes..."

"Okay. When is your father's birthday?"

"Well, it is May 4th."

"Perfect. Today is March 30th. You have enough time to enjoy Tokyo in 1985. But you have to leave before your father comes into this world."

XXIII

Gunié learned later that *Gunié* was not originally from Japan but a country from Central Asia.

"Let me explain," said *Gunié* and started drawing a figure.

"There're 3 types of time travel. Number one, vertical time travel, from 2020 to 1985 from Tokyo to Tokyo for example. Number two, horizontal time travel, from Tokyo to my place.

Number three, diagonal time travel, from Tokyo in 2020 to my place in 1985. Right? I used to choose diagonal one because it is the fastest method. But a

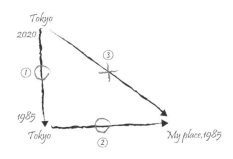

diagonal time travel requires tremendous amount of energy so now I never use it."

"But wait," Gunié interrupted, "I understand you need a vertical time travel plus a horizontal time travel so you can come back to the original place, the original era. But is the second one really a 'time travel'? Because you just move from 1985 to 1985. Do you know what I mean?"

Gunié looked at Gunié in astonishment and then shook his head, smiling.

"Good question, Gunié, but horizontal one is also a time travel. You don't have to understand. What you have to know is you're such a smart girl."

XXIV

Gunié knocked the air four times with his right hand and a familiar capsule appeared. When he rubbed the surface of it with his palms, the capsule became 20 times as big as the original size.

"This is your mini room, Gunié," he said.

"I need to time-travel back to my place where the language you don't understand is spoken. You stay here and explore the city, OK?"

"Okay... but I'm a bit scared of being alone."

"No worries, smart girl. If you run into trouble, call me by shouting '*Ezmwa Ezmwa*'. I'll come here right away."

Gunié snapped both of his fingers three times and crouched with his eyes closed. After a few seconds, he disappeared without making any noise.

XXV

Biro's mission as a clown at Cirque de la Nature was to perform a double-back somersault in artificial lightning, which was extremely dangerous. Even if the lightning was fake, he needed to become accustomed to a powerful electric shock. And that was why he always carried the metal kit.

Although the circus did not have chances to hold a show due to COVID-19, the members of Cirque de la Nature regularly needed to gather and practice their own performances.

On his way back from the training hall, Biro dropped by his high school just to make sure it was closed. It was the first week of April. Under ordinary circumstances, the spring vacation would be over within a couple of days. He walked again and headed for his home.

Soon after he came back, Biro accessed to the high school's internal website to check its coming schedule. No information was updated. Then he noticed that an internal social networking platform had been launched within the site. He entered the platform by clicking the main button. There were many Q&A rooms such as 'Math Q&A Room' or 'Geology Q&A Room'.

"Maybe they'll start online classes before long," murmured Biro.

When he was about to exit from the platform, he spotted 'Lost & Found Room'.

"Well, why not? Let me try this," he said to himself.

XXVI

Biro entered 'Lost & Found Room' and posted a message, asking if anyone was looking for a medium-sized egg-shaped openable item.

He accessed to the room on the following day. There was no reply.

He accessed to the room again after three days. He did not receive any messages.

"Um, I need to change my strategy."

Biro clicked a new message button and typed, "I'm looking for a girl called Maja. She is around ten years old and may live near Ueno Station."

On the following day, he accessed to the room and found a message to him, saying, "Maja is my younger sister's name. She goes to elementary school. Our house is close to Ueno Station."

The sender of the message was Agira Ibamoto.

XXVII

Soon after *Gunié*'s departure, Gunié went into her mini room and immediately fell asleep on the sofa. She slept for hours and hours.

She woke up the next day at around noon and remained motionless with a drowsy face for a while. Then she remembered what had occurred the day before.

"I'm in 1985..."

She looked around the room. There were many 500-yen coins on a small table. She counted them.

"...thirty, thirty-one, thirty-two... It should be March 31st today, so..."

Gunié came to the conclusion that she would survive unless she spent more than 500 yen a day.

Gunié got out of the room and headed for Senso-ji. The Kaminarimon – the entrance gate of the temple – was full of people. She passed through the gate and walked westward along Kaminarimon-dori Avenue. She walked and walked until she found Zaitoh family's house.

"It's the same, but it's new!" thought Gunié.

Suddenly, the door of the house opened and a woman came out. She was expecting a baby. Gunié hid herself in a hurry.

"She must be Grandma and Dad's in her big tummy!"

XXVIII

There were so many discoveries in 1985. Above all, vending machines were much bigger! And nobody carried a mobile phone. Some people seemed to be talking through a big green phone in a tiny transparent room on the roadside. When Gunié went to a convenient store and bought an onigiri, she paid only 100 yen and not 110 yen.

About a week after her arrival at Tokyo in 1985, she decided to go to the Tokyo National Museum and walked to Ueno Park. There were numerous people picnicking in the park. The cherry blossoms were in full bloom.

"Another Hanami season this year. How lucky I am!" Gunié shouted with sparkling eyes.

XXIX

Biro and Agira met in front of their high school and headed for Ibamoto family's house. According to Agira, his sister had been shutting herself up at home for more than a week.

"My little sis is quite a fan of Cirque de la Nature. She may get a bit of energy back if she sees you," said Agira.

Maja was in the living room watching anime.

"Hi, Maja. Enjoying TV?" asked Biro.

She looked back to him.

"Who are you?"

"You'll see who I am," said Biro and threw a somersault on the spot.

"Biro Biroda?" said Maja with a faint smile.

"Why are you here?" she asked.

"I have some questions about the item you took to the kōban."

She put a dismal look on her face.

"The man Gunié met at Ueno Station was you..."

It took Maja a while to start talking about what had happened to her on the 30th of March.

XXX

"Did Gunié disappear? Are you serious?" asked Agira half-excitedly.

Maja nodded and burst into tears.

"No worries, Maja. Gunié didn't disappear. I guess she used a special trick," Biro tried to calm her.

"How do you know?" Maja continued crying.

"Hey, I got it!" Agira interrupted suddenly.

Biro and Maja looked at him.

"Raise your hands and shout the secret word here now, Biro. That's the trick. In this way you may be able to meet her. What's the word, Maja? Was it '*Rubberducky*' or something?

"'*Nabberyocky*'. But don't do this, Biro. I never want to see someone disappear in front of me again."

"But wait," Agira insisted, "the word is the biggest clue and the fastest manner to solve the mystery, right? If you disappear, it means her trick was successful and so is yours. You catch up with Gunié, and take her back to this place. And everyone will be happy."

Biro thought what Agira had said made sense.

"OK, Agira. I'll have a go now."

"Good luck, dude," said Agira.

"No! Don't go, please!" cried Maja.

"Don't worry, Maja. I'll be back as soon as I can," said Biro. Then he raised his hands and shouted, "*Nabberyocky!*"

XXXI

The three were in the same living room.

Nothing happened. There was an awkward atmosphere among them.

"Alright. Let's switch to plan B," said Agira.

"Plan B? You mean, I need to try '*Shabberwocky*', too?

"Be realistic now, Biro. Let's go to Gunié's place and talk with her family. We can even borrow '*Gunié in Wonderland*'

from them. The book might have some hints."

"Say it from the very beginning," said Maja and Biro almost simultaneously.

XXXII

Dagaji was working online when the three children paid a visit to his place. When Maja saw him, she started crying and said repeatedly, "I'm so sorry, Papa Dagaji. I'm really sorry..."

"We apologize for a sudden visit," said Agira, "but we'd like you to give us any information on Gunié's whereabouts."

"We also want to borrow '*Gunié in Wonderland*' from you awhile," Biro added.

Dagaji looked around them slowly.

"Don't cry, Maja. Gunié should be okay and will be back," he said.

"From where?" asked Biro.

"I don't know. Time will tell," replied Dagaji.

"But we do want to know the truth as soon as possible and we might get some clues if we traced what Gunié have read. Can't we borrow the book?"

"No, Biro," Dagaji shook his head, "Gunié is now on an adventurous journey. If you want to follow her, don't rely on the book. You must do it in an adventurous way."

All the three children thought Dagaji knew where Gunié was. On their way back from his house, nobody said a word until Biro and Agira broke the silence at the same time.

"What I don't understand is..."

The two boys looked at each other.

"Go ahead, Biro. I guess we want to say the same thing."

"Okay. What I don't understand is why Gunié's father

seemed so relaxed. He should be upset in this situation."

Agira shook his right index finger, tut-tutting.

"Well, that's not what I was about to say, Biro. It was natural for Papa Dagaji to behave that way in front of us. He's a grown-up man, you know?"

Biro thought Agira had a point. Dagaji might have tried to hide his shock.

"You may be right, Agira. So what did you try to say?"

Agira gazed at Biro for a moment and tilted his head to one side.

"What I don't understand is why Papa Dagaji knew your name."

XXXIII

On the 16th of April, Gunié noticed at Asakusa Station that the minimum fare for the subway was not 170 yen but 120 yen.

"Even if I bought a ticket twice, I would spend only 240 yen. 500 minus 240 equals 260... Maybe I can survive with a remaining 260 yen today."

She looked at a big subway map above the ticketing machines, and decided to buy a ticket to Kanda Station. At the ticket gate of the Ginza Line was a man with a black hat. He had something

like scissors in his right hand. Gunié got scared. What if she got questioned by the man? Keeping a sufficient distance, she observed the gate. He did not seem to be a policeman. Gunié tried to mimic what other passengers did and passed through the gate

successfully.

Not so many passengers were on the train. Some were reading a book or a manga, but most of them were sleeping on the seats. She got off at Kanda Station, went up to the ground level, and walked northward along Chuo-dori Avenue. Gunié went on walking straight, but when she caught sight of Akihabara electric town in the distance, she turned left and kept walking.

XXXIV

Nothing along Yasukuni-dori Avenue really interested her until she spotted a huge bookstore on the left side. The store was called Sanseidō. She entered the building and explored the shop. There were a tremendous number of books and magazines inside. Gunié found some attractive books but knew she could not afford them.

"Well, I'll come here again after I go back to 2020," she thought.

Gunié took the exit on the other side of the building and

walked along Kanda
Suzuran-dori Street,
where there were quite a
few small and medium-
sized bookshops. After
walking for a minute or
so, Gunié got a sense of
déjà-vu. Wondering
when she had been there
before, she kept going
and spotted a familiar
bookshop on the right

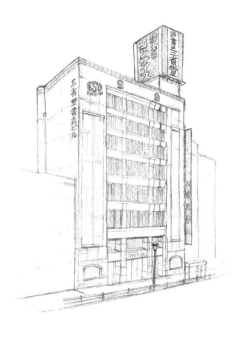

side of the street: 'Bookworms' Paradise'.

XXXV

Gunié entered the 'Bookworms' Paradise'. Although it was
not so big as Sanseidō, it had as many books as 35 years 'later'.
Behind the cashier counter was a young man reading a book, not
paying attention to the visitors.

Gunié was curious if the shop already had '*Gunié in
Wonderland*' in 1985. She looked for the book for a while in

vain, so she decided to talk to the young shopman.

"Excuse me..."

The man looked at her. He had dark green eyes.

"At your service, Mademoiselle," he answered politely.

"Do you sell '*Gunié in Wonderland*' here?

The shopman frowned. "We do have 'Alice in Wonderland' but not '*Gunié in Wonderland*'. Never heard of the title."

He stared at her suspiciously but soon changed his facial expression to a smile.

"I'll track our inventory anyway. Who is the author, please?"

"It was... it was written by Shusha Dao," replied Gunié sheepishly.

The young man rolled his eyes and said to her in amazement.

"Shusha Dao! That's my name!"

XXXVI

Gunié appeared just in front of Gunié immediately after she shouted '*Ezmwa Ezmwa*'. She was sitting on a bench in the park near Jimbo-cho.

"What's the matter, Gunié?"

"I, I got lost, and..."

She told him what had happened at 'Bookworms' Paradise' and added that it was the bookshop where her father had bought '*Gunié in Wonderland*' for her birthday.

Gunié listened to her carefully and stared thoughtfully at Gunié.

"To be honest, I didn't know until now such a book exists," he said.

"You didn't know? No way. You're the protagonist of the book," she claimed and added, "besides, if it was not you, who drew a correction line on '*Shabberwocky*' and wrote '*Nabberyocky*' on the book?"

Gunié did not answer her question and held his own head with both hands with his eyes closed. He seemed to be trying to remember something.

After more than a minute, he opened his eyes and said, "I'm afraid I don't know what's going on, Gunié. But I know there's one thing we have to do."

"What do we have to do?"

"We have to tell Mr. Dao to write '*Gunié in Wonderland*'."

XXXVII

"I knew you'd come back here sooner or later," said Shusha Dao to Gunié, "but not this soon."

"We're sorry to disturb you again, Mr. Dao," said *Gunié*.

"Call me Shusha. What are your names?"

"Gunié," she said.

"*Gunié*," he said.

The shopman looked at them with amazement.

"Are you siblings?"

"No, Mr... well, Shusha. We happen to have the same first name."

"I see. So what do you guys want me to do?"

Gunié cleared his throat before he began speaking.

"We'd like you to write a novel based on our stories."

Shusha remained silent with his right hand on his chin. After a short while, he looked up at them and opened his mouth.

"Sure I will. Why not? But not today. Come to this shop at 8 a.m. from tomorrow. You'll have one hour to tell me your stories each time. Deal?"

XXXVIII

Biro was in front of his PC at his place.

"What does Gunié's father know and why didn't he allow me to read the book?" he wondered.

He searched for '*Gunié in Wonderland*' on the Internet, but nothing came up. No information on either '*Nabberyocky*' or '*Shabberwocky*' was found.

"Gee, I'm totally stuck!," he said in a loud voice and pounded his fists on the desk. He glared at the calendar he had taken from the item angrily.

All of a sudden, Biro noticed that Coming-of-Age day fell upon Tuesday, not Monday.

JANUARY						
SUN	MON	TUE	WED	THU	FRI	SAT
		1	2	3	4	5
6	7	8	9	10	11	12
13	14	15	16	17	18	19
20	21	22	23	24	25	26
27	28	29	30	31		

"Oh, this calendar is not correctly printed..."

He tried to reach out for a calendar, then abruptly shuddered.

"This is not a calendar of 2019..."

He flipped the January page slowly and looked at the February page. Nothing was strange. He continued. The March page was okay, too.

"I'll check all the pages, anyway," he thought and flipped it.

When Biro looked at the next page, he found that the 29th of April was 'The Emperor's Birthday'.

"This is a calendar of the Shōwa period."

He grasped one of the 500-yen coins inside the item like a bull at a gate. It was a memorial coin for the International Exposition held in Japan in 1985.

XXXIX

"Gunié went to the year 1985!"

Biro was at Ibamoto family's house. He told Agira and Maja that all the things inside the capsule-like item were related to that year.

"To be honest, your idea is too fanciful," Agira pointed out, "I think this is a carefully crafted prank. Someone buried the item with 1985 stuff in Senso-ji. And Gunié and you, Maja, you were successfully fooled. Gunié is probably staying safe somewhere now in 2020 but can't go back home for some reason."

"But I saw Gunié disappeared in front of me. If she was safe, she would have contacted me by now," insisted Maja, "as you say, Biro, she must have gone to 1985..."

Biro tried to put his thoughts together. "If it is really a prank as Agira says, who planned it and for what purpose? Where's Gunié now? What does her father know? Why did I have to get involved? Is it because I always carry this metal kit...?"

"By the way," Agira broke the silence, "1985 is the year when Marty McFly accidentally went to the past."

"Marty what?" asked Biro.

"McFly. He's the protagonist of a film titled '*Back to the Future*'," said Agira with a smug face.

Biro nodded with no interest.

"And did he return to 1985?" It was Maja who showed interest.

"Yeah. He made it after twists and turns."

"How?"

"He used a lightning strike."

XL

Biro was in the training hall for Cirque de la Nature, waiting for his turn. He was nervous but was determined to shout a magic word while doing a double-back somersault in artificial lightning. His only concern was whether he should shout '*Shabberwocky*' or '*Nabberyocky*'. The latter would lead him to where Gunié was, whereas he might be able to meet *Gunié* who should know Gunié's whereabouts if he shouted the former.

His turn came before he made a final decision. Biro stepped forward to the stage, squatted on his right heel and on his left knee, placed his right arm on his right knee and his left hand on his left thigh, and closed his eyes. The practice started with a usual sound of thunder, followed by lightning.
He jumped up and shouted at the same time, "*Shabberwocky!*"
That moment, a huge noise echoed throughout the training hall and Biro vanished. All the other members of the circus thought his performance had been unsuccessful.

XLI

The rumor of Biro's disappearance spread throughout his high school immediately. But Ibamoto siblings did not believe that he had burnt out in the middle of lightning but that he had gone to 1985.

"Biro was right. Gunié time-traveled and he followed her," said Agira.

"We've got to go to Cirque de la Nature office and tell them what's happened to him," said Maja in a firm tone.

"Who'll believe he went to the past while we have no proof?"

Maja shrank back.

"Er, what should we do now?"

"I don't know. We have no choice but to wait," Agira sighed.

"I shouldn't have taken Gunié to the Five-Story Pagoda," Maja started blaming herself, "I shouldn't have told you and Biro what had happened. I should've stayed here in this room instead of visiting Papa Dagaji..."

"But wait," Agira interrupted.

"What?"

"Let's speak with Papa Dagaji. Good job, Sis!" He patted

Maja's head.

XLII

Dagaji was not home, though.

"Do you want to leave him a message?" asked Zaori.

"Thank you, Mama Zaori, but we'll come again tomorrow."
Agira said so and was about to bow to her.

"By the way, Papa Dagaji left a message to you."
Both Agira and Maja blinked in surprise.

"What is the message from him?"

"He said you must avoid non-essential and non-urgent outings under a state of emergency. Come here again in the second half of Golden Week."

"Why does he...?" murmured Agira.
Maja started sobbing.

"But we came here because this is an urgent matter. Papa Dagaji doesn't understand how serious the situation is."
Zaori gently tapped Maja's shoulders and smiled at her.

"No worries, Maja. Everything will be fine after a couple of weeks."

XLIII

Every morning Gunié rode a portable bike she had been given from *Gunié* and headed for 'Bookworms' Paradise'. *Gunié* always waited for her sitting on the doorstep of the shop. The door opened at eight o'clock sharp and Shusha beckoned the two storytellers to enter the shop.

Gunié told Shusha about what she had read and what had happened to her. *Gunié* sometimes helped Gunié clarify her explanation or gave additional information, but most of the time he served as a listener. Shusha wrote down everything he heard from them without showing any expression on his face. When the alarm clock rang at nine o'clock sharp, he put his fountain pen on the table and said, "I will see you again tomorrow morning."

Gunié always went back to Central Asia soon after the morning routine.

"I'll come here and wait for you no later than 8 a.m. tomorrow," said he in front of 'Bookworms' Paradise' and disappeared.

Gunié spent the rest of the day hanging around the districts

between Jimbo-cho and Asakusa or taking a nap in her mini room.

"Boring," she thought.

XLIV

Only one week was left before Gunié's departure from 1985. As was usual, she spent an hour at 'Bookworms' Paradise' together with *Gunié* and Shusha.

"I think we've told you all the experiences we had," said *Gunié*, "do you need any other information? Otherwise we won't come here tomorrow to disturb you."

"I do," replied Shusha, "I need to know what will happen to you from now until your return to 2020. You don't have to come here everyday, but come to this place just one day before you leave, which is... May 3rd. Deal?"

"You're not coming here until the 3rd of May, are you?" asked Gunié to *Gunié* with an anxious tone of voice.

He smiled at her and said, "don't you want to see Fei Fei and Huan Huan?"

"Sorry?"

"Fei Fei and Huan Huan. They're giant pandas. If you want, let's go to the Ueno Zoo to see them now. This is well-earned reward for your good job in the last ten days, Gunié!"

XLV

Gunié left the Ueno Zoo with *Gunié* and walked eastward, holding an ice-cream cone in her hand.

"Can I ask you a question, *Gunié*?"

"Yeah, go ahead, young girl."

"Well, why were you chosen to be a time traveler?"
Gunié watched her with admiration.

"Good question, Gunié. But to be honest, I don't know why I was chosen. A messenger came to my place and said so."

"A messenger!" said Gunié excitedly, "is he also a time traveler?"

"She," he corrected, "yeah, I guess she is. But I have never seen her since then."
When Gunié was about to ask him another question, someone suddenly tapped her on the shoulders and said, "finally, I've found you, Gunié!"
She made a weird face and looked back.

"Do you remember me?"

Biro was standing just in front of her.

XLVI

"So you are Biro! Nice to meet you, I'm..."

"*Gunié*, right? I was looking for you, too. Good to see you at last!"

The two boys shook hands. Gunié looked at them and thought they resembled in appearance.

"How did you come here? Did anyone help you time-travel?" asked Gunié.

"Actually, I made it by myself. I used a lightning trick and came here successfully."

Gunié rolled his eyes.

"It's almost a miracle you didn't get electrocuted."

"Well, I'm a kinda used to electric shocks," said Biro.

"I see... But never do it again. It's too dangerous," warned *Gunié*.

"Okay. Are there any other dos and don'ts I have to follow?"

"Oh yes," said *Gunié*, "you have to be careful not to see yourself or your family here in 1985. How old are you?"

"I'm seventeen."

"Alright, no problem. Were your parents already born in 1985?"

"They must have already been born. Biro's older than I," interrupted Gunié and spoke to Biro, "does it make sense?"
Biro remained silent for a short while and said, "you don't have to worry about my family."

"Why?" asked Gunié.

"Because I've never seen my parents."

XLVII

Biro told Gunié and *Gunié* that he had been brought to an orphanage at the age of two and stayed there until he turned twelve years old.

"Isn't there a possibility that you're Biro's dad, *Gunié*?" Gunié asked a question without thinking it through.

"Why do you ask me such a mysterious question?" *Gunié* asked back.

"Because...," Gunié stammered, "because I thought you

look somewhat alike."

"Listen, Gunié," said Biro with a furious tone, "I've never seen my father but I know what happened to him. *Gunié* can't be my father. Period."

"I, I'm sorry, Biro. I really am. I didn't mean to offend you..."
Her slip of the tongue created an uncomfortable atmosphere for a moment.

"Biro's right. I can't be his father. Do you know why, Gunié?" *Gunié* cut through the silence.
She shook her head.

"Because I am much older than you imagine."

XLVIII

"As I told you, Gunié, I became a time traveler when a messenger came to me. It happened when I was fifteen. Since then I never get old," confessed *Gunié*.

"And you've served as a time traveler for how long?" asked Biro.

"Almost eighteen years. I was born in 1952."

"15 plus 18 equals..., so you're 33 years now in 1985 and,

and in 2020 you'll be... very old!" Gunié gave up calculating his future age.

Gunié smiled and said, "Shusha's right. We need to take you, Biro, to his place before your departure and introduce you to him."

XLIX

Gunié made another mini room for Biro on the other bank of the Sumida River. He created a bike for him, too.

"By the way, Biro, you can stay here as long as you want since you don't have a family-related issue," said *Gunié*.

"Oh, can I?" said Biro, but soon continued, "but no, thank you, I'll go back together with Gunié. I promised Agira and Maja to take her back."

Gunié showed a satisfied expression on his face.

"I'm happy to hear it, brave man. I know Maja's Gunié's best friend and Agira's her brother, am I correct? And remember, Biro, you'll have to tell Shusha what you talked, what you did, and what you promised with the siblings."

"Who's Shusha, by the way?" asked Biro, "why does he need to know what happened to me?"

Gunié tried to soothe Biro's mind by talking to him as slowly as he could.

"Shusha is a man who has to write '*Gunié in Wonderland*'. You already heard about the book, didn't you?"

L

Gunié came to Tokyo to see Gunié and Biro every morning. He thought Gunié was still a little nervous about being with Biro alone, and decided to serve as a mediator until their return from 1985.

His concern turned out to be futile though: the two soon felt comfortable with one another. Gunié looked happy to have a companion to kill time during the day, and took him to several places she already knew. Biro who gave up the life counting on smartphones and computers

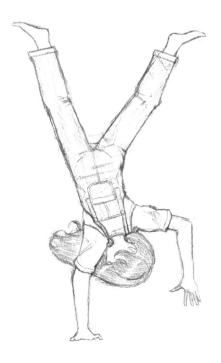

enjoyed teaching her how to do acrobatic feats such as a cartwheel or a split leap.

It was already the 30th of April. As was usual, *Gunié* came to Tokyo and spent a couple of hours with them and left the place saying, "I'll come here again tomorrow morning."
He did not appear on the following day, though. But Gunié and Biro did not take it seriously.

"He's probably busy," they thought.
Gunié did not appear on the 2nd of May, either. They started to get anxious.

"We're supposed to go back the day after tomorrow. What if *Gunié* doesn't come here by then?" said Biro with a worried voice.

"We must trust him," said Gunié firmly, "let's do what we've got to do before he's back."

"Well, what do we have to do?"

"Um..., we have to buy some souvenirs for Maja and Agira. And, oh yes, I need to get a birthday present for my dad."

"I don't think you can take the things of 1985 to the future. We need to ask *Gunié* before our departure. What else should we do in advance?"

"Oh, I totally forgot about it!"

"What?"

"We have to meet Shusha tomorrow at eight a.m. sharp!"

LI

"Did you put something on your face, *Gunié* ?" asked Shusha.

Biro paused awkwardly, then said, "I'm not *Gunié* actually. I'm Biro Biroda and I've come from 2020 just like Gunié."

Shusha gave Biro a long look with his dark green eyes.

"I see. You resemble him anyway. Is one hour enough for you to tell me your stories?"

Biro and Gunié left 'Bookworms' Paradise' and headed back for their mini rooms by bike. They went to a department store named ABAB on their way, and Gunié bought a handkerchief for Maja, a towel for Agira, and a message card for Dagaji.

Gunié was at the exit of the department store, waiting for them. He seemed exhausted.

"You did see Shusha, right? Sorry I didn't make it," he said.

"Are you alright, *Gunié*?" asked Gunié, "you look pale."

"I'm okay, but I have to go back soon. I've come here to tell you about tomorrow's schedule."

"OK," nodded Biro and Gunié simultaneously.

"You have to get up very early tomorrow morning. Leave your rooms as they are and go to your grandparents' house, Gunié, at half past six."

"Too early! Why do we have to hurry up?"

"Because your father is expected to be born at seven."

"Oh, by the way," interrupted Biro, "Gunié has just bought some gifts for her friends and father. Can she bring them to 2020?"

Gunié cast apologetic eyes at Gunié.

"I'm afraid you cannot take anything to your family."

She dropped her shoulders in disappointment.

"I bought a message card for his birthday..."

"I'm really sorry, Gunié. But if you want, you can give the card to your father in 1985 instead. Write a message and leave it in your grandparents' mailbox.

LII

Biro got up at a quarter to six on the 4th of May, 1985. He soon left his mini room and went to Gunié's mini room. When he reached, she was already awake and ready to leave her room. They walked westward and arrived at the house of Gunié's grandparents at around six twenty. Gunié dropped her message card into the mailbox.

Gunié appeared in front of them at half past six precisely.

"Ready to go back?" he asked.

"I'll miss you, *Gunié*," said Gunié, "but come to 2020 again soon."

Gunié smiled sadly and nodded.

"We didn't have much time to talk face-to-face this time. But let's do it when I see you next time," suggested Biro.

"Yeah, let's do it sometime somewhere."

"Now, stand here side by side," said *Gunié*, "don't say a word anymore, OK? Close your eyes and never open them until everything is over."

Biro and Gunié acted as was instructed. Then *Gunié* put his right palm on Gunié's forehead and his left palm on Biro's. The two voyagers stood still, waiting for a magic word to return to 2020. Suddenly, they felt something very hot inside their bodies. Without listening to any magic words, they lost consciousness.

LIII

"Welcome back, courageous adventurers!"

Gunié and Biro opened their eyes and saw Dagaji in front of them.

"Dad, I'm... I'm...," Gunié did not know what to say.

"Enter, enter. Breakfast is ready. You must be hungry now."

LIV

Gunié and Biro gobbled down the breakfast without a word: they had not realized that they were so starving.

After they finished with their meal, Dagaji brought '*Gunié in Wonderland*' and put it on the table.

Gunié burst out in tears.

"Sorry, Dad. I'm so sorry..."

"You're sorry for what, my dear?" asked Dagaji.

After crying for a minute or so, she started speaking.

"No, nothing. But yes, happy birthday, Dad, but I have no presents for you."

Dagaji smiled and said, "just a moment. I'll get some stuff to show you."

"It's here." Zaori showed up with something in her hand.

It was a message card Gunié had dropped into the mailbox 'thirty five years ago'.

Welcome to this world, baby Dagaji.

I will see you very soon and

Happy Birthday ! :)   Gunié☆

"You knew everything!" said Biro, "that's why you looked so calm."

"Not really," responded Dagaji, "I knew something, but not everything. We just believed we would see you again."

Gunié got overwhelmed by what was happening in front of her. She was left speechless with her mouth open.

"Are you alright, Gunié?" asked Zaori.

She was broken from her trance and picked up '*Gunié in Wonderland*'.

"One more sorry, Dad. I broke my promise. I said I'd finish reading this by today, your birthday."

Zaori and Dagaji looked at each other, then smiled at Gunié.

"Don't worry. The stories from the chapter 10 to the chapter 17 are about your adventures, Gunié and you, Biro. But you will need to read the chapter 18, the final chapter today if you want to keep your promise.

LV

Chapter 18

On the 30th of April in 1985, *Gunié* went to Tokyo as was usual, stayed there for a few hours, and came back to his country. He had an appointment with Gublai, the head of time travelers, on that day.

"Fine. What do you want to know?" asked Gublai. *Gunié* needed to confirm if it was okay to have two persons time-travel at once.

"The number of the persons itself does not matter," said Gublai firmly.

"Happy to know it won't be harmful to them. That's what I..."

"The problem is," Gublai cut in, "you already made the girl travel twice."

"What do you mean? Will the third travel be hazardous to the girl?"

"No. She will not be in danger at all."

"So, what's the problem?"

"The problem is, it will put your life at risk."

Gunié was ordered by Gublai to learn more advanced method to time-travel: the one which would not bank on magic words. It might still put his life at risk, but it was much safer than the conventional method. The training was hard since the new technique required as much energy as a diagonal time travel. But he practiced and practiced, and finally mastered it one day before Biro and Gunié's departure.

"Good job, *Gunié*. You need to sleep a lot and store energy tonight," said Gublai.

"I will, Gublai. I have to go to Tokyo now but will be back as soon as possible."

When *Gunié* was ready to leave for Tokyo on the 4th of May, Gublai appeared in front of him. He had an envelope in his hand.

"If your attempt is successful, this is going to be handy for you," he said and gave the envelope to *Gunié*.

"What's inside?"

"Open it after you send your friends to 2020. Good luck and see you later."

Gunié arrived at Gunié's future house at six thirty,

where the two voyagers were waiting. He was tensed up, but tried to hide his agitation.

"I'll miss you, *Gunié*. But come to 2020 again soon," said Gunié.

"Let's talk face-to-face more next time," said Biro. *Gunié* wondered if he would survive and see them again.

"Now, stand here side by side," said *Gunié*, "don't say a word anymore, OK? Close your eyes and never open them until everything is over."
Soon after Biro and Gunié closed their eyes, he put his palms on their foreheads. Then he closed his eyes and concentrated his whole attention on his heart so it would generate special energy. When he felt there was sufficient amount of energy inside his body, he transmitted it to their bodies at a stroke. At that moment, *Gunié* got a terrible headache and collapsed on the ground.

Gunié regained consciousness and looked around. Biro and Gunié were not there. He stood up and tapped his own cheeks a couple of times.

"I'm alive...!"
When he was about to walk away from the place, he

heard a baby crying.

"Gunié's father has just been born," he thought.

He arrived at Ueno Station and sat on a bench. His next mission was to dispose of two mini rooms, but he was too tired to go to the Sumida River from there.

"Excuse me, sir."

Gunié looked up. A woman with a suitcase was standing in front of him.

"Yes?"

"If you know, could you please tell me how to go to Ryokan Sawanoya?"

He had no idea where it was.

"I'm sorry, but I'm not familiar with this area."

"Oh, it is fine. Thank you anyway, sir," said the woman and went away.

"Sir?" wondered *Gunié*, "why did she say 'sir' to me?"

He walked to an advertising stand with a mirror nearby and looked at himself.

"Gee..."

He became eighteen years older.

Gunié sat on a bench again and opened the envelope Gublai had given to him.

No sooner did he find a passport, some 10,000-yen

bills, and a flight ticket to Central Asia in the envelope than he realized that he lost his power to time-travel.

He went to Narita International Airport on the same day and left for his country.

The End

LVI

Agira and Maja came to Zaitoh family's house in the afternoon.

"I really missed you," said Maja and hugged Gunié tightly.

"Welcome back, Biro. You made it, dude," said Agira.

Gunié gave a handkerchief to Maja and a towel to Agira.

"These are old, but brand new," she said with a mischievous grin.

Maja gazed at Gunié with her wondering eyes for a moment.

"But you look different, Gunié."

"Do I?"

"That's what I thought," interrupted Agira, "you look grown up!"

"She is," said Biro, "besides, she is fitter now. Show them what you can do, Gunié!"

She nodded and turned cartwheels on the scene.

"Bravo!" Everyone applauded.

LVII

After Ibamoto siblings left for home, Gunié, Biro and

Dagaji went to 'Bookworms' Paradise' in Jimbo-cho. Gunié wanted the shop to keep the book so that other children could read it.

Behind the cashier counter was a middle-aged gentleman with a mask and glasses, reading a book. He looked at the guests and stood up.

"Good evening, Monsieur."

"Good evening, Mr. Dao. And thank you so much for your message a month ago," said Dagaji.

"Mr. Dao?" said Gunié and Biro and looked at the gentleman.

He took off his glasses and watched them with his dark green eyes, smiling.

"Shusha!" shouted Gunié with an ear-to-ear grin.

Once in every three or four years after 1985, *Gunié* visited Shusha's bookshop and told him about his adventures. In 1988, he went to Cairo by airplane to find a time capsule he had hidden inside the Great Pyramid of Giza. In 1991, he traveled to Rome to find another capsule inside the Colosseum. He told the stories about his 'non time-travels' to Paris, Agra, New York, Rio de Janeiro, Berlin, and Sydney. He said treasure huntings were always exciting, and getting older was enjoyable.

"Does he still visit you?" asked Biro.

"Not since five or six years ago," replied Shusha, "he must be busy."

"I want to see him again. Where are you, *Gunié? Ezmwa Ezmwa*!" shouted Gunié desperately.

"No, Gunié. He's lost all these kinds of ability," said Biro.

"Next time he comes here, I'll let you know."

"Thank you Mr. Dao," said Dagaji and continued, "we must go now."

Shusha looked at Biro and asked, "what are you going to do now?"

Biro gave a slight shrug.

"I don't know. Perhaps I'll contact my high school and my circus after Golden Week is over."

"Stay here tonight. There is a small room upstairs. It was a long day for you and you, too, Gunié. You must get a good rest."

EPILOGUE

That night, *Gunié* appeared in Biro's dream. He was encompassed with a dense fog and hard to see, but he looked like an old man.

"Hey, *Gunié*! We've talked a lot about you this evening."

He gazed at Biro with unblinking eyes, saying nothing.

"Are you okay, *Gunié*? You look bizarre. Is there any..."

"I have come here," *Gunié* suddenly began speaking.

"Pardon?"

"I have come here as a messenger to notify you that you were chosen to be a time traveler, effective immediately.

To be continued by

'Biro in Wonderland'

Special Thanks to :

Biro Biroda

Taro Fukano

Gublai

Gunié

Daichi Hayashi

Agira Ibamoto

Maja Ibamoto

Ayumi Kato

Kento Kento

Rei Kokubo

Marty McFly

Gonko Nanashi

Kuniie Shizuku

Heizo Yamazaki

Dagaji Zaitoh

Gunié Zaitoh

Zaori Zaitoh

Gunié in Wonderland

2023年3月24日　初版発行

著者　　　　雫　洲舎（シューシャ・ダオ）

発行・発売　株式会社三省堂書店／創英社
　　　　　　〒101-0051　東京都千代田区神田神保町1-1
　　　　　　Tel：03-3291-2295　Fax：03-3292-7687

制作　　　　プロスパー企画

印刷／製本　藤原印刷